Bully Proof Life

The ultimate action plan for kids and their parents, so we can create a new generation of superheroes

By
Chris Casamassa

Table of Contents

Introduction

Creating the next generation of superheroes is our mission, our passion, and our purpose. Our goal is to help train, inspire and educate 1 million kids to become more confident, more focused, and more bully-proof than ever before.

The battle against bullies has been going on for generations. Since the 1960s, the number of children experiencing bullying and are reporting instances of bullying behavior has nearly quadrupled.

Kids and parents will be better equipped to combat this with time-tested and proven strategies to fight back against the dangers of bullying.

Our step-by-step system has already helped over 100,000 kids get stronger, feel safer, and become more confident. Getting kids BULLY PROOF helps them feel better on the inside and look better on the outside. According to many studies, a lack of self-esteem is the number 1 cause of bullying.

Legal and Copyright

Bullyprooflife.com
364 W. Foothill Blvd.

Glendora, CA 91741
info@businesskombat.com

Ordering Information:
Quantity sales. Special discounts are available on quantity purchases by corporations, associations, and others. For details, contact the publisher at the address or email above.

Printed in the United States of America

First Edition

Meet Chris Casamassa

Chris Casamassa is a lifelong martial artist. He is currently a 9th degree Black Belt and CEO of 14 Red Dragon Karate schools in Southern California, founded in 1965 by his father Louis D. Casamassa.

With over FOUR decades of experience, Chris is widely considered an expert in martial arts. HE specializes IN KID'S safety and health.

Chris wrote the original #1 bestselling book *Bully Proof Fitness*: *The Ultimate Guide for Parents in the Battle against Bullies and Bellies and How to Make Your Kids Feel Like a Super Ninja.*

He has appeared in dozens of films and TV shows, including his portrayal of the iconic ninja Scorpion in the *Mortal Kombat* franchise.

For more about Chris, visit: www.chriscasamassa.com

Testimonials

"Chris never ceases to amaze me with his ability to connect with people, making it easy and fun to learn how to handle bullies. He may play the role of a superhero in movies, but he truly is a hero for kids and adults who have ever been bullied. Learn from his expertise and watch your kids become bully proof!"

Bedros Keuilian,
Founder of Fit Body Boot Camp

"I have been practicing family medicine for over 30 years. Since meeting Chris over 20 years ago, I have witnessed firsthand how he has made a difference in our younger generation with his teachings. As a martial arts professional, he has demonstrated time after time that he is a thorough, caring, and intelligent professional. His knowledge and insights in getting kids bully proof and fit are without equal. Kids need to be fit. In addition to benefiting their general health, it also makes their mind stronger and more confident. I highly recommend his teachings and the advice in this book."

Dr. Cris Armada, Jr., DO
Armada Wellness & Family Care

"Chris Casamassa is the country's champion, as a four-time #1 North American Sport Karate competitor. Chris is *my* champion because he plays Scorpion in all the *Mortal Kombat* movies and TV shows I produce.

But these things are not what really convinced me Chris is a champion, in the true sense of the word. Something else did. Here's the story.

We had a launch party for the first *Mortal Kombat* movie. One aspiring martial artist/wannabe actor cornered Chris and rambled on and on, bragging about how he could kick anyone's butt, his style was the best, and he was the toughest guy there.

Now, this guy had no idea who Chris was. Neither guy had any idea I was listening.

But Chris did not brag. He did not interrupt. He did not point out the ridiculous nature of all the things the wannabe tough guy talked about. He did not embarrass the guy as he easily could have. Chris politely stood there, listened, nodded, and simply let the guy finish. Then he moved on.

Then I *knew* that Chris is a real champion. One who knows it and doesn't have to prove it to every insecure dude out there. He's a real champ who doesn't need to show off and lets his actions speak, not his words.

From that moment on, Chris and I have been friends. He's been in lots of our productions. He hosts a popular show on our network, Blackbelt TV. He is slated to play a lead in one of our upcoming movies.

He is always enthusiastic, full of ideas, and creative ways to help and make things better.

To find someone in the movie business talented in martial arts and acting is rare.

To find someone like that who is also classy, humble, and helpful – as Chris is – is almost impossible.

So here's the deal. This book will help your kids. This book will help the world because bullying sucks, and he can help negate it.

But here is the surprise – this book will also help *you*, no matter who you are. Learning from the mind and soul of a true champion – of which there are precious few in the world – is priceless."

Larry Kasanoff
Executive Producer
CEO of Threshold Entertainment
Santa Monica, CA

Bullying Defined

There are a million ways that kids and adults can be bullied. In the interests of clarity, we have divided them into sub-categories. Also, as the most significant focus of this book is on school-age kids, we'll refer to the bullied as "students" from now on.

Verbal: the student is called names or teased in a hurtful way. Within this verbal section, we also have *Rumors,* in which the student is the target of exaggerated stories or outright lies.

Exclusion: the student is left out on purpose or completely ignored.

Sexual: the student is bullied with words or gestures having a sexual meaning

Racial: the student's race is the focus of the bullying

Physical: the student is hit, kicked, pushed, or has their personal property stolen or damaged

Cyber: the student is bullied online, via a mobile phone or another electronic device

Kids are most often bullied by being called mean names, having false rumors spread about them, or being left out on purpose.

Within our Bully Proof Life program, there are a series of different challenges that we take kids through during our live training.

Typically, we cover sections 1-3 the first time we visit a location and then sections 4-7 the second time we visit.

Regardless of which stage or section we are in, we *always* start by getting them to understand the most common words that are most associated with this subject.

When we say understand, we do our best to make sure they know the word's MEANING and not just a surface definition. This allows us to dive deep into their psyche and can help kids grasp the subtle differences between intent and action.

In our Bully Proof course and live event programs, we ask the kids to define the key words we discuss, such as **Bullying**, **Violence**, **Respect,** and more. We ask them to tell us what t*hey think it means.*

This is important because asking them for **Their answers** instead of us just "lecturing" them on word definitions makes a huge difference. This holds their attention in what we are doing and aids their retention of what we covered. The students remember more of what we teach versus any other type of program.

We *need* the attention of students because the topic is critically important. Of course, we want them to retain what we teach after we are gone.

As a bonus, any parents in attendance at our live events also know that we're training the kids to have an intuitive understanding of our topic in their minds. I know this may sound obvious to most adults, but having trained over 71,034 kids at this point, you would be surprised by the answers we get when it comes to defining these words.

The interactive part of this word definition section is fun, as we ask for volunteers to come up and help.

Our live demonstrations are instrumental in really driving home the lessons. They allow kids to quickly grasp the true meaning behind a word. As we will repeatedly discuss throughout this book, it also helps them "course correct" themselves when they engage with our demonstrations.

It is incredible to see the "*aha!*" moment on the faces of the kids when they begin to realize they may have been exhibiting bully-type behaviors. Oftentimes, they had no idea they were heading down the wrong path.

In the live action sessions, we perform real-world examples of the four main types of Bullying behaviors. As a reminder, these are:

· **Physical**

· **Verbal**

· **Relational**

· **Cyber**

In each of the sections, we ask the kids leading and open-ended questions about what they just saw. This type of interactive training has proven itself to be the best way for kids to learn how to become BULLY PROOF for LIFE

Bully Proof Life event at Oak Mesa Elementary School in La Verne, CA

Physical Bullying

Characteristics of a bullying situation include:

- Imbalance of power

- Intent to harm

- Worsening over time

- Terror or fear in the child being bullied

- The bully enjoying the effects of the action

- Implied or explicit threat of further aggression

When I travel the world doing our Bully Proof events, we start by asking one question – "who thinks they know what the word BULLYING means?" Not what it *is,* but what it *means.*

Typically, we get common answers. Teasing, making fun of somebody, pushing them, stealing ... all the playground classics.

Of course, those are all great answers ... until we hit them with the truth:

"Bullying is any behavior that intentionally humiliates or harms another person."

So, we take single individual answers – teasing, pushing, stealing – and create an entire world of understanding for the kids in one sentence.

But….

That's not enough.

Quickly, they begin to realize that it's not a *single* thing that defines bullying. Instead, it is a sum of all actions taken together.

We go on to explain. If you're making fun of someone, although you're not maybe hitting them or pushing them, you're still on the path to being a bully. If you're truly friends with someone, you lift them up, you don't knock them down. If you have friends who are constantly making fun of you or teasing you, those aren't your friends.

Too many kids believe, or don't know, that if one, two, or three kids are messing with them, teasing them and pretending to be their friend … they are *not* a friend. We explain to them that is *not* what real friends do. Real friends build you up, support you, and laugh WITH you, not at you.

We also remind them that at their school, there are hundreds of kids. If one, two, or three are making them feel bad, they can – and should! – find new friends that won't bring them down.

We appreciate that this can sound intimidating, especially for kids. As a result, we show them easy, fun, and effective strategies they can use to make new friends.

A series of events are then played out when we ask for "volunteers." In this section of the Bullying definitions, we ask kids to come up and be the "star."

This means interacting with us, not just sitting and passively listening. This helps kids become part of the show and help other kids – their peers – learn.

It is important to note that MOST kids are kinesthetic learners. This means they learn by *doing*, not just watching and listening. At the end of the day, that's what we are there to do – to make sure they learn in a fun way that will be remembered long after we have packed up and left.

It's also way fun for them to see their classmates go up against the "big bad karate master!" For example, in the physical bullying segment, we will walk by the volunteer child and "accidentally" shoulder bump into them. We then get the other kids in the audience to respond to the question: was I a bully?

The most surprising part is the number of "no" responses we get in the beginning. This is the start of the self-realization – that there is much more to this Bully Proof Life than they thought.

Here's a description of how we play that out for them. I walk by our volunteer and bump his shoulder with mine. I then ask all the kids, "was I being a bully?"

At this point, many of them have a correct answer of yes. I try and make it more challenging for them by saying, "come on! I *barely* touched him!" Minimizing impact and trying to shift the blame onto the victim is a classic bully tactic.

I then ask them again – was I a bully or not? We get the kids to "vote" yes or no. Of course, we give them big hints by saying, "*from here on out, don't let me trick you.*"

The answer, of course, is yes – I *was* a bully. We then explain why. In this example, I had plenty of space. I didn't need to touch him. In fact, it would probably have been easier to just walk on by.

Even if I couldn't – let's say he was close to a window or wall. We explain that, if I needed to pass him, I could have easily asked him to let me by, then thanked him when he did so. To just barge on past, bumping him on purpose, is 100% the behavior of a bully.

At the end of this book, there is an incredibly easy and effective bully proof self-defense move that any child can learn in less than 10 minutes

Verbal Bullying

Defining physical bullying is pretty obvious. In our second example, though, we need to get a little more subtle to challenge the mindset of the kids in attendance. Again, we ask all the kids to see if they can identify if I am a bully, this time based on words rather than actions.

Step one is to bring another volunteer up, get right up in their face, and say to them, "when this class is over, I'm gonna kick your butt."

Clearly, 100% of the kids get it. This is a classic form of verbal bullying. We congratulate them on their success at identifying that behavior and quickly switch gears.

Using the same volunteer, I say – in a very sarcastic tone – "hey kid, nice pants" – and then ask who thinks that I am a bully. Usually, at least 50% of the kids get this wrong. I let them know that, once again, I'm 100% being a bully.

I explain why. I just made fun of his clothes. We talked about behavior that humiliates, which is a form of bullying. If I say "nice pants," I know I don't really mean it. I'm trying to make fun of him in front of others. I intentionally made fun of him to try and make myself look cool.

But ask yourself – how does he feel after a comment like that? Built up or torn down? At this stage, the kids are on point and really start to grasp the concept. So, I ask again – does making fun of somebody's clothes make me a bully or a hero? They know and they tell me emphatically.

We end this section of the training by saying (again) that our job is to lift people up, to make them feel better about themselves. That when we do so, we can create a generation of superheroes – *not* super-bullies. Superheroes lift people up, while super-bullies try to tear people down. Your mission is to be a superhero.

We also teach them real-world "how to" techniques, such as:

- How to react if a bully does this to you

- How to ensure you don't do that to somebody else

- How would you feel if you saw someone to that to one of your friends? More importantly, how would you react? What WOULD you do?

- How to deal with – and what specifically to say – to a bully when they are teasing you

- How to verbally de-escalate any threats or intimidating actions a bully will take towards you.

It's important to note that when the kids watch us *demonstrate* bullying, they understand it much faster than if we were just simply lecturing. In addition, we constantly reemphasize to all the kids to watch closely to see if these are the type of things they are unconsciously doing right now. These are the actions that could be placing them on the path to becoming a bully, and we don't want that to happen.

Our goal is to help raise a generation of superheroes, not a generation of superbullies.

Relational Bullying

Relational bullying is the #1 thing that gets the biggest reaction – and trips up most kids. This is most prominent when they realize they are potentially just as guilty as the primary bully.

The theme here is simple – "if you say nothing, you're just as bad as the bully."

Here is the demonstration. We bring up volunteers again – in this case, three kids. Our volunteers and I form a semi-circle so we can play catch with a ball. We then get another volunteer kid to approach us and ask, "can I play with you?"

In this scenario, I always act as the bully, so I simply say. "No, we're good, we have enough people" - and continue to throw the ball to the other kids until the "victim" volunteer walks away (usually sadly!)

We immediately stop the scene and ask if I was a bully. The kids, of course, loudly resound with **YES**. Then I ask if any of my friends were being bullies, to which they reply **NO**. Occasionally a few kids catch on and say yes, but this is rare.

After the shock of me telling them they are wrong wears off, I explain why. If this ever happens with any game, if somebody comes over asks to join in, the answer should be yes. I appreciate that team sports generally need a balanced number, but we're talking in generalities here – the answer should never be no.

Get free training and bully prevention resources at www.bullyprooflife.com

Here is the big takeaway, though. If you let me – the bully – use my relationship with you – other kids – to exclude somebody, you are just as bad as me.

We then replay the scene. Here is where the power of interactive bully proof training comes full circle. 100% of the time, it plays out completely differently – and this time, correctly.

The volunteer child approaches and asks to join in. The answer from me is the same – "no, we have enough people, leave us alone." The difference is, the other kids shine, quieting me down and literally drowning me out, inviting the volunteer to play.

Like any bully, I don't give up easily. To their credit, the other kids have now formed an alliance against the main bully. So much so that, eventually, it is *me* that walks away dejectedly. It gets even better, because at this point all the other kids who were watching erupt into spontaneous applause.

Doing the right thing is *always* the right thing to do. This is a powerful lesson that, once taught and instilled at an early age, is how real-life superheroes are created.

Cyber Bullying

Now, I think we can all agree that bullying in ALL its forms is wrong. Cyber bullying, however, is the weakest, wimpiest, and most cowardly of all forms of bullying, in my view.

With cyber bullying, there is no real-world confrontation. In essence, there is no real-world danger for the bully. This can make them feel even more entitled, emboldened, and empowered. A very dangerous combination when used to bully others.

These keyboard cowards can hide in a small corner of their mom's basement, typing all sorts of nonsense and untruths, and then send their poison out into the world. At least with physical, relational, and verbal bullying, there has to be some semblance of face-to-face interaction.

During the COVID 19 pandemic of 2020 and into 2021, we were forced to go online if we wanted any kind of friendly human interaction beyond our immediate family. In the wake of that, social media and online interaction are at an all-time high.

With the tremendous rise in the use of Zoom and many other group meet-up platforms, this technological shift made all of us, young and old, even more enveloped – and, dare we say it, proficient – in our online interactions. We now can quickly and easily connect with our friends and family around the globe.

That rise in and of itself does not make the world of social media evil or dangerous. The internet as a whole is neither good nor evil. It is ambiguous. It's the people who use the thing in one way or another that create what we experience.

Kids can and should use the internet to interact with others. To seek and gain knowledge as *a part* of their entire life experience. Unfortunately, the internet and social media can become dangerous and addicting for kids – and adults! – when they spend "too much" time online.

The term "too much" is in quotes because there is no perfect amount of time for any expert to recommend. If you Google, "how much time should my kids spend online?" you will find as varied as a response as asking, "how much should I invest in bitcoin?" Everybody has an opinion, and none are more valid than any others.

Time and use guidelines when it comes to the internet and social media are a parental responsibility. Every child is different, and as parents, we are supposed to know our kids best. For better or worse, internet time-watching is now a mandatory and important part of our parenting job.

There are kids who should be online, there are kids who can be online, and there are kids who should *not* be online. There are kids (and parents) who can easily become addicted to the internet.

As a parent, I can tell you the very general rule I use. When they would rather stay online than go outside, it's too much. When they would rather stay online with their friends instead of actually *being with* their friends in person, it's too much.

As a parent, I treat it the same way I would treat any other addiction. If it's the thing they want to do as soon as they wake up, or instead of any other normal human interaction process, it's a problem. We need to pay close attention to our kids and their behavior.

This is, of course, an oversimplification of a very complex parenting issue. This is why we, as parents, need to educate ourselves. Congrats on doing so by buying this book! More information can also be gained by using the internet as a source of good and downloading our app.

There's a flip side argument to be made here, too. I know I may potentially lose some parents here, but it's important to understand that cyber bullying in and of itself isn't a phenomenon of social media. Cyber Bullying is a phenomenon of parents creating a false reality for children.

Here is a small sample of what I'm talking about. 8th place trophies, graduation parties when they move from 3rd grade to 4th. Telling them they are still the best when they lose, coddling them at Every. Single. Turn....

Look, I get it. I'm a parent too. We want our kids to be safe. We want them to be protected. We want them to NOT make the mistakes we made... I get it.

But when you are trying to get them to avoid *any* pain, struggle, or hardship, you are doing them a disservice. You are actively teaching them to be average and mediocre. You are moving them farther away from greatness. The struggles, the defeat, the pain, all of it – these things forge character, make us stronger, and teach skills that lead to success.

Of course, *do* tell your kids that you love them. Tell them that you are proud of their efforts. Tell them you know they will do better next time. Just be wary that constantly sheltering them from real-world problems at every turn doesn't help.

Letting kids quit a sport or activity because they lost, or it got too hard, or they aren't playing as much as the other kids ... that doesn't help raise a superhero generation. It weakens them. It disables them from understanding how to overcome the adversity that life will surely throw at them.

For our kids to be brave, to stand up for themselves and for others, we parents need to avoid being overbearing and overprotective. We need to be guides in their life journey, not directors or event dictators.

Superheroes go through many ups and downs. They face struggles, they overcome challenges, and they become brave, courageous, and resilient as a result. They learn to make the right choices without us.

Yes, of course, it depends on their age but those of you who "helicopter parents" know who you are and what I'm talking about. It creates a false sense of entitlement in kids and can force them to look for the wrong people in the future. People who will continue to tell them only what they *want* to hear, not what they *need* to hear.

This is where online (and real-world) predators live. In this false dream world, where it's all good, where everything will be OK. Just let me whisper everything positive that you want to hear into your ear, and I'll immediately gain your trust.

Kids need a little conflict. They need to lose before they can win. They need to learn that failure and defeat are part of the game called life. No champion at anything – whether it be sports, art, finance, business, or technology – won all the time. Nor were they told losing was OK.

They were taught how to get better, how to pull themselves up, and how to remove problems when they arose. How to dig deeper to find their true purpose. When the world as a whole embraces this, not only will kids become better the world itself can be a much better place.

Rant over. Now, **let's get back to cyber bullying**.

We are not just going to look at the negative. There is a strong positive to the world of online interaction. Look at the number of kids who are happy today at 11, 12, 13, or 14 because they can chat with their friends on IG, Twitch, or Snapchat. A decade ago, these same kids would've been miserable, sick, or depressed because everyone at school messed with them, and they didn't have an outlet or somewhere to go to find their own tribe or better friends.

This has helped, and *is* helping thousands of kids, to NOT commit suicide, to not run away from home, to not withdraw from family and friends. There are clear health benefits of being part of an online community.

One of those benefits has to do with emotional wellbeing. Online social networks have become a pervasive part of everyday life. They are revolutionizing the way we spend our time, communicate with others, and maintain social relationships. These networks allow users to keep in touch with friends, increasing feelings of social capital, and they also have extra benefits

Here are three positive effects of social media on your mental health from an article by Kevin Naruse at www.paintedbrain.org, a company that specializes in helping others

1. Social Media Allows You to Connect With Family and Loved Ones

We are social beings that long to socialize, interact, and connect with others. Social media allows you to stay in touch with your loved ones promoting positive mental health.

Elderly individuals and people with limited mobile mobility particularly benefit from social media platforms, as they get to connect with loved ones without the need to travel.

In a recent survey, where 1,000 pensioners were surveyed, the findings indicated 7 out of the 10 surveyed seniors used Facebook to connect and keep in touch with loved ones. For such people, interaction through social media helps prevent loneliness and depression, among other mental health issues.

2. Raises Awareness on Mental Issues

Through social media, organizations and individuals can raise awareness of mental health issues. This has also seen social media become an important learning tool that inspires healthy lifestyles.

For instance, unique hashtags can make a mental health issue trend on Twitter. Instagram can also be used to spread positive and helpful hashtags that touch on mental health issues.

In one such awareness post, an organization shared a picture of an egg on Instagram to create awareness on mental health. That photo of an egg that received more than 52 million free Instagram likes and was at one point the most-liked photo on the platform.

The organization later posted a cracked egg, noting that the egg cracked due to pressure from the overwhelming attention it received. Alongside the cracked egg was a message for people who feel under pressure to seek help. A powerful visual image and message.

Mental health organizations on Instagram can also help people who appear to be struggling with issues such as suicide, depression, and more. The site also has a self-injury reporting tool that can help reach out to people who may be struggling with a mental health issue.

3. Source of Social Support and Interventions for Mental Health Issues

An increasing number of online groups and websites are offering mental health support through social media. Such sites provide hotlines for suicide prevention, anonymous forums, and SMS services to help those with mental issues on their recovery journey.

Through such platforms, people with mental health issues can seek help anonymously. Many young people can also now post personal issues on online support groups and forums, something they wouldn't do with their parents or close friends.

This makes early interventions to such issues possible. Such anonymous sharing also encourages self-expression and minimizes the danger of stigma.

In one study, researchers Eva C. Buechel and Jonah Berger found out that socially apprehensive people may find refuge in social media when they need to talk to someone. They go on to suggest that online social networks have become extremely popular, one of the most popular features of online social networks, microblogging (e.g., tweeting or sharing Facebook status updates), is driven in part by its undirected nature.

Microblogging allows people to simultaneously express themselves to a sizable number of potential communication partners without having to address anyone in particular.

As a result, this communication channel is particularly valued when people feel socially apprehensive; it allows them to reach out without having to impose communication on a one-on-one basis. They conclude that these findings help to shed light on one reason why people use online social networks.

Contributing to this debate, Buechel and Berger suggest that a unique feature of these networks can actually offer a valuable outlet for expression and social sharing. One of the most popular features of Facebook, and the hallmark of Twitter, is the broadcasted sharing of short messages (i.e., status updates or tweets) about thoughts, feelings, or actions with other users who can read them and respond. While Facebook status updates and tweets vary in a number of ways, academics and practitioners alike collectively call such short messages "microblogs."

Microblogging is immensely popular. Each day there are over 500 million tweets and more than 125 million Facebook status updates. The study same study by Buechel and Berger also found that microblogging can be valuable to kids and teens who may be struggling with social interaction.

Microblogging increases opportunities for desired social interaction. Microblogs vary from other communication channels in important ways. They differ from face-to-face interactions in that they are written and in that, they do not require making eye contact.

Microblogs also differ from face-to-face and other forms of communications (e.g., texting, emailing) in that they are *undirected.* Initiating social interaction usually involves directed communication: reaching out to particular individuals and thus imposing social interactions onto them.

Imagine you're at work and want to connect with others. Before online social networks, you'd have to stop by someone's office or call them on the phone, both of which involve reaching out to a specific person who might feel obligated to respond. Similarly, sending emails or messages to one or more people usually requires directing communication at selected recipients who might feel they should respond. All of this can feel difficult, especially when people feel socially apprehensive.

In contrast, by offering undirected communication, microblogs reduce the burden of bothering any particular person while still offering the possibility of social interaction. While different online social networking platforms differ in many ways, both status updates and tweets go out to a large number of online ties in an undirected manner.

If the undirected nature of microblogs can facilitate sharing, as they suggest, then microblogs should be particularly valuable and useful when people want to reach out but feel socially apprehensive about doing so. The experience of social apprehension should increase sharing via microblogs because their undirected nature enables desired social interaction while minimizing anxiety about burdening others.

Their conclusion is that social media can positively impact your mental health. But to enjoy these benefits, you should limit the time you spend online and also focus on using social media for the right reasons.

Alas, not everybody will use social media for the right reasons. During our bully proof training course, we teach, discuss and help kids with cyber bullying and the use of social media in our live Bully Proof for Life course.

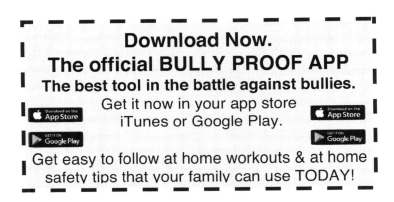

Bringing out my own cell phone, I ask the kids, "how many of you sitting here before me have one of these?" Many hands go up. I then ask, "how many of you have a tablet or a laptop computer?" Everyone in the class has raised their hand at least one time. Some of them raised their hand *every* time. To which I say with a smile, "oh my, you are all so spoiled."

I then tell them, "this part of the bully proof class is not a test for you. It's a test for your parents." This is the part where many of the parents get a little nervous! I say, "if you can finish my sentence, you have great parents. If you cannot, I think I need to go have a private conversation with your parents."

Ready to take the test yourself?

All right, finish this sentence.

If you don't have something nice to say....

99.9 % of all kids can finish this sentence easily. To which I respond, "I knew you all had great parents, look at you." To which many of the parents will breathe a sigh of relief.

I go on to explain and continue to get the kids to finish a new sentence – "If you don't have something nice to write…"

They respond quickly: _Don't write it."_

Here's the final point on cyber bullying. I tell the kids, point blank, "in my opinion, the weakest and most cowardly form of bullying is cyber bullying."

Again, in the interests of clarity, _all_ forms of bullying are wrong. To bring this full circle from earlier in this chapter, at the very least with physical, relational, and verbal bullying, there has to be some semblance of face-to-face interaction.

These "keyboard cowboys" hide in their basement in the dark, typing, texting, and tweeting all kinds of nonsense that just isn't true, and then without any filter, they just send it out into the world. That is what makes cyber bullying both dangerous and cowardly.

In conclusion, continue to be good parents. Do monitor your kids' time online. Keep being a leader and role model by example for your children. You can do this!

Fear, anxiety, & depression should never be part of a kids world

*Sources: (Ellison, Steinfield, & Lampe, 2007; Hoffman & Novak, 2012), (Buffardi & Campbell, 2008; DiSalvo, 2010; Forest & Wood, 2012). (Kraut et al., 1998; Tonioni et al., 2012; Turkle, 2015).(Kaplan & Haenlein, 2011; Lee, 2011; Walasek, Bhatia, & Brown, 2018) Kevin Naruse www.paintedbrain.org, **Eva C. Buechel**,& **Jonah Berger** Journal of consumer psychology 2017*

Defining Violence

In this section of the live course, we help kids understand key words. Words that they hear all the time but may not be fully aware of what it means for them in cases of potential bullying.

Violence is a word we hear a lot. But do we really know what it means? By definition, violence is simply <u>the use of force to create fear.</u> When we cover this word in the course, there are two sides to violence – victim, and victimizer.

We use illustrations here, designed to create what we call a "lightbulb" moment. These help kids realize that the things they may be doing – whether at home or at school – have the potential to lead them down the wrong path.

The kids who are starting to head down the victimizer path need to learn and understand how to "course correct" their behavior with the help of their parents' nurturing and positive reinforcement.

Sometimes when you talk about the word violence and what it means to kids, there is nominal impact. During our live demonstrations at Bully Proof Training, though, you'll see the kids physically react as they realize, "oh, wow, he's not kidding, I really do behave that way sometimes."

We demonstrate by bringing a volunteer up again. Typically, I use a small piece of paper rolled up into a ball and throw it like a pitcher in a baseball game at the child. Then I'll ask the kids in the audience, "was I being violent?"

Most of the kids will say no. It was only a small piece of paper, after all. The correct response, of course, is yes, though. I ask them, "what if that paper was a rock? What if that paper was an actual baseball? Would I have been violent then?" This is when the a-ha responses start.

The point for the kids is it's not so much *what* I am throwing, but *how* and *why*. What is the intent behind what I'm doing? By throwing anything, I am physically and deliberately trying to create pain in someone else and make them afraid. In doing so, I am **using force to create fear.**

In this case, we're trying to help kids realize that any action that is not done out of kindness, love, or respect can be seen as violent and is always the wrong choice. Kids that throw things at each other, even if it is a simple piece of paper, begin to realize that they are possibly moving down the wrong path. That this could be seen as exhibiting violent behavior.

Just to make sure, I quickly add, "wait a minute. It was only a *piece of paper*, for Pete's sake! How violent could that really be?" Here's what's good about our live demonstration. The kids catch on. They're learning. Fast. They still say yes.

Next, we ask the kids again using a different scenario. The second part is that I wind up the "paper ball" and throw it hard, directly at the ground, in front of the volunteer. Then we ask again – "am I being violent?"

Most of the kids are quick to say yes, but some are still not sure and answer no. I explain, although I didn't hit the volunteer, the act of me winding up hard and fast and then throwing the object near their feet typically gets a bigger fear response from the volunteer. As a result, this is still an act of violence.

You can see the difference. When I throw it at the volunteer the first time, they don't move too much, but when I get to this second part, and they've been hit once, things change. My volunteer flinches a lot and looks more afraid than when I threw it directly at them.

We quickly ask the kids again, "what is the definition of violence?" They answer in unison, "the use of force to create fear."

So, when I ask if I was violent once more, by 'just' throwing a paper ball at the feet of somebody with force, they understand that the answer is still a very loud yes.

Now that they have the right answers and understand the definitions of bullying and violence, we can move on to something a little more fun and entertaining. The next section of bully proof training enjoys a welcome assist from the "Queen of Soul."

Respect

Let's talk about how Aretha Franklin helps kids of all ages be the most respectful people in the world.

As we are all aware, respect is part of the golden rule – *"Treat people the way you want to be treated."* Parents all over the world tell their kids this. Sometimes the kids get it, and sometimes they don't.

There are a couple of causes that lead to this. One – and this might sting a little – is they hear mom or dad say, "treat people the way YOU want to be treated" – but they don't SEE it or experience it at home.

This confuses kids and leads to incongruences that can haunt them for the rest of their lives. If you are married or single with kids, make no mistake. Kids learn a lot more and much faster from SEEING and from experiencing versus the verbal word. It is also one of the reasons why our live classes are always so much more impactful on the kids understanding respect.

The second potential cause of children not treating people the way they want to be treated is peer influence. Who they hang around with socially or at school has almost as much impact as what they see and hear at home. An old saying that claims we are the sum of the five people we spend the most time with.

Think about that in your own life for a moment, and you will see how true that statement is. We are all influenced by those we spend the most time with we can be influenced in a positive way or a negative way.

This includes the time you spend with "friends" online or even something as seemingly mundane as watching the news on TV. Is there ever anything good or positive on the news? This is an industry with the saying "if it bleeds, it leads."

So, it's important to limit the time you spend with the people or things that makes you unhappy. Of course, this is sometimes hard. When it's a parent, boyfriend, girlfriend, another family member, or a job that is getting you down, it's not easy to just walk away. The more you chip away at it, though, the happier you will be.

This is what *really* matters in the game of life. We get only one spin around this planet; why live miserably? A not-so-gentle reminder for all the parents. Your kids are watching you and learning from you even when you say nothing. Our actions as parents are often stronger and louder than our words could ever be.

I know what you're thinking now, though. What does all of this have to do with Aretha and respect? We're getting there…

In the class, we tell the kids everything you just read. We challenge them to find better friends but NOT in the way you might think.

Here's how that plays out. I ask the kids who is ready to be the best superhero, and all their hands shoot up. I tell them that great I'm so excited for you to take on this job to find better friends and be a leader at your school. Then I assign them the following assignment.

"The next time you go to school, I want you to find the kids NOBODY is talking to. The kids that others say are 'weird' or 'strange.' I want you to have the courage to go over to that kid and ask if you can sit with them or ask them if they want to come to play with you and your friends."

That's what the most respectful superheroes do. They help lift other people up.

You see, anybody can choose to hang out with the 'cool' or popular kid. It takes a real superhero to go find the kids that maybe lack a person to lift them up – and to be that person.

What happens today, affects them in all their tomorrows.
BULLY PROOF FITNESS

When I ask kids if they can do that, they never hesitate to shout yes. At that moment, they learn how leaders lead by example by showing respect and kindness to others.

I know what you're thinking. "Cute story Chris, but I'm still waiting to hear that this has to do with Aretha. You better not be taking her name in vain."

Well, after we talk to the kids about respect and how best they can show it, I set them another challenge. I make it pretty clear that we take this challenge seriously – usually, I'll add, "if you get this one wrong, you will not pass this class, and you cannot get your graduation ribbon."

The kids are on edge. They have been actively engaged, and they want to pass. I ask them to spell respect, and they think I've set an easy one, but I have a trick up my sleeve.

Yes, Aretha fans, this is where the Queen gets her due. I tell the kids that I taught classes all over the world, and nobody kid has ever gotten the spelling of this word correct. I plead with them to be the first group to get it right. I then grab a dry erase marker and a board and ask them to spell the word respect.

We do this one letter at a time. They start to shout out.

R

E

S

P

E

C

T

Like a game of *Who Wants to be a Millionaire*, I ask if this is their final answer. They reply in the affirmative, and I fake utter disappointment when I tell them they are wrong.

The kids look at each other and their parents with curious gazes. The parents start to wonder just who let this illiterate fool into a school.

That's the point that we announce that there *is* a way they can pass the class. It involves learning how to correctly spell the word RESPECT. We also tell them that after they learn this 'correct' spelling, they will never forget it.

We then go into our best karaoke version of the classic song *Respect* by Aretha Franklin.

First, they have to raise both hands and lean to one side. Then we have them repeat after us. We get the kids to sing along with us and have a great time. And a result, they haven't just learned how to be bully proof – they have also learned the lyrics to a classic song.

Mastering Your Emotions

When you realize you control your mood, everything gets better. There is an old saying that applies to martial arts, business, and just about any aspect of our lives – never let your emotions outweigh your intellect.

If you are a younger person reading this, that may not make much sense now, but it will.

Emotions are a powerful force. Wars have been started because of emotion. Heck, kingdoms have risen and fallen because of emotion. For example, Queen Louisa of Mecklenburg – the wife of King Frederick William of Prussia – pressured her husband into a war against Napoleon after Prussia's would-be allies, Russia and Austria, had already been defeated.

Consider the Trojan War, too. This was a famous conflict between ancient Greece and the city-state of Troy, now located in modern-day Turkey. Helen was a Greek princess betrothed to the king of Sparta, Menelaus, but secretly had an ongoing affair with Paris, prince of Troy. The conflict began when Paris abducted Helen on the night of her wedding and escaped with her to Troy. They did *not* live happily ever after.

This list can go on. By now, though, you see that getting an emotional response – good or bad – can be a very powerful thing indeed.

Modern day advertisers know this. That is why any successful ad you see is designed to evoke an emotional response:

See if you can recognize these slogans:

- Just Do It.

- Think Different.

- Where's the Beef?

- Open Happiness.

- Because You're Worth It.

- Melts in Your Mouth, Not in Your Hands.

- A Diamond is Forever.

- The Breakfast of Champions.

Answer key: Nike - Apple -Wendy's -Coca-Cola -L'Oreal -
M&Ms -De Beers -Wheaties -

Controlling your emotional anger is an important part of staying bully proof.

There are a few verbal and mental word techniques we teach the kids to help combat their emotional responses throughout our course. This way, kids learn how to assess how they are feeling – and gain a sense of the emotional state of their potential adversary.

They learn to say:

- This too shall pass

- I'm OK; this will get better

- 3-2-1 breathe

And other mantras.

We hope you see how much *you* can control and endure unwelcome emotions during challenging times. It's critically important to always look for nonviolent solutions to the things you don't control.

One more takeaway. Don't overvalue somebody else's opinion. This is especially important when they don't know you, but it even applies to your closest family and friends!

When somebody has an opposing viewpoint, take it in. Understand it. Empathize with it. Just don't put that opinion on a pedestal. When you're kind and have good intentions, you're always on the right path. Remember, doing the right thing is always the right thing to do.

And speaking of right … let's get back to parenting 101. Two wrongs don't make a right. I'm amazed by how many people hear this – and *know* this – but do not heed the advice. It's important to stop combating bad behavior with bad behavior.

Kindness is always the answer. Empathy is a great way to place yourself in someone else position and imagine for a moment what they might be going through *before* you throw a punch in their face.

Instead of battling anger or resentment with more of the same, throw love and compassion at them. When you do so, you'll stun them for the win in life. And maybe, just maybe, they'll stop and think twice about behaving this way in the future.

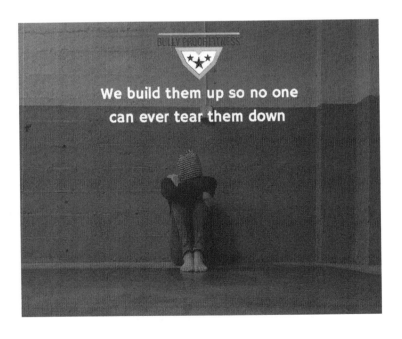

Telling vs. Tattling

Before we dive into this chapter, let's ensure we understand the difference between aggression, conflict, and disagreements.

Conflict is simply a disagreement or difference of opinion or interest between equals.

People who are involved in the conflict may disagree, and emotions may run high when conflict is badly managed. This, in turn, can result in aggression – though it does not need to.

In a conflict, both parties have the power to influence the situation. Ultimately that's their goal. It's important to understand the difference between conflict and bullying.

You cannot use conflict resolution techniques on somebody that is being bullied. Imagine asking a student that endured months or years of bullying to face their tormentor to explain the impact of their actions.

That may sound like a good idea – it may be good for the bully to learn some home truths. The trouble is, the victim is then expected to listen to the perspective of the bully or the tormentor.

Maybe this will be a therapy session that ends in handshakes and hugs, and everybody feels better. Alternatively, maybe the bully just shrugs and says they pick on the victim because they *can* – they do it because they're bigger and stronger, come from a richer family, or just don't like their face.

When a bully is unrepentant, conflict resolution just will not work. All you'll do is make the victim feel worse about themselves. This is why it's important to understand the difference between simple conflict and outright bullying.

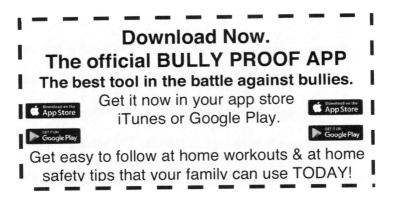

Now, for kids to understand and recognize the difference between bullying and conflict behavior, they also need to learn the difference between tattling and telling. This is especially in younger children.

There are a plethora of movies and TV shows that convey kids being called a 'tattletale', 'rat', 'snitch', or 'cry-baby.' This can leave children, especially when young, afraid to do the right thing and tell adults what is happening.

If you break it down, the difference between tattling and telling is pretty simple.

Tattling is something you do to get somebody in trouble, usually for no big deal.

For example, imagine a brother and sister – let's call them Johnny and Susie – are in the living room by themselves. Susie yells, "Mom, Johnny's looking at me funny!"

Well, that's just tattling. He's not really hurting her. He's just looking at her.

Telling, on the other hand, is getting help when you know somebody or something could get hurt, or harm could arise. Now *that* is important.

Let's return to our kids in the living room. If Johnny approaches the open fireplace and starts playing with matches, trying to set a piece of paper on fire, that's clearly dangerous.

If Susie says, "Mom, Johnny's trying to burn paper in the house," that is telling. In that instance, *not* saying something is the wrong thing to do. It is critical that kids understand the difference.

While that's a pretty simplified explanation of the difference, it's important for children to be able to understand tattling versus telling.

Tattling is just telling on someone in order to get them in trouble for no apparent reason. Telling is something _you need to do._ You tell an adult or a teacher that someone or something might be getting hurt or badly damaged, or someone's rights are getting infringed upon.

Kids should be able to be strong and safe and not be afraid of telling versus tattling.

References: from www.safeatschool.ca. A bullying and prevention website designed to help students understand bullying conflict and the differences between them.

The F.B.I. Did It

Why is it important for students to be fit and safe, and learn how to protect themselves physically?

An FBI report entitled, _The Indicators of School Crime and Safety_, provides data on crime and safety in schools from the perspective of students, teachers, and principals. It's an annual report from the FBI Law Enforcement Bulletin.

The report contains 23 indicators of crime from a number of sources, including the National Crime Victimization Survey and the School Crime Supplement to the Youth Risk Behavior Survey.

Topics covered include victimization at school, teacher injury, bullying, and cyber bullying, school conditions, fights, weapons, and student use of drugs and alcohol.

The report also lists student perceptions of personal safety at school. The FBI report contains these important highlights.

1. Students aged 12 to 18 experienced approximately 1,420,900 non-fatal victimizations at school, including 454,000 thefts, and 966,000 violent crimes

2. Nearly 22% of students between 12 and 18 reported being bullied at school, and 7% reported experiencing cyber bullying during the school year.

3. According to the most recent data, 15 homicides of school-age youth, between the ages of 5 to 18, occurred at schools.

4. 33% of students reported fearing attack or harm at school, or on the way to and from school.

5. Almost all students between the ages of 12 to 18 observed at least one security issue at their school.

Those statistics alone should be enough for any parent to want their kids not only to be fit but to be able to protect themselves, to walk without fear, to be able to be aware and focused on what's going on in the world around them.

What's Up, Doc?

Doctor Don Pet M.D. is the #1 bestselling author of the book *Seven Word Switches to Happiness, Love and Peace: Loving Yourself with Abundance That Overflows to Enrich the World.*

I had the opportunity to talk to Dr. Pet at a conference in San Diego, California, on kids and the power of early development. When I asked him about the importance of confidence and self-esteem and its importance in kids' lives, here's what he had to say:

"There are seven simple words that we can teach, and two very simple love creation skills that are not only appropriate for the kids but they start with the parents."

We found that getting kids into shape and giving them confidence – specifically *self*-confidence – is one of the most important things that we as parents can do for our kids. Kids that do not have self-esteem are such easy targets to their peers. It's so important to them.

They're very simple. You can take these seven words and put them on one piece of paper. If you learn them and practice them regularly, they become automatic and effortless within 30 days. From then, they will last forever.

The first one is when you say **I think I can** instead of **I can't, I give up**, or **why bother**. "I think I can" is like a word switch that turns on our energy. Think about *The Little Engine That Could*. We all know that story, the kids love it. It was one of my favorite stories.

The little engine was asked to take the toys over the hill to the people who deserved them because the big engines were too busy. They were too proud to do that. The little engine had never done this before, but he said, "I think I can, I think I can."

Before you know it, he was over the hill and acting with real bravery. We need to start off by turning our energy switch on to the positive belief if I can.

Our second word is **I allow** instead of **they make me.** "I allow" says I am going to take responsibility for myself instead of blaming other people or blaming myself. When we blame ourselves, we call it guilt. When we say *I* allow instead of *they*, *he*, or *she*, we get rid of the guilt and blaming. It's among the most important things any of us can do.

The third word is **I could** instead of **I should**. "I could" says that I'm gonna ask myself what choices I have. "I should" suggests that we are basically doing what somebody else told us was the right way when we were growing up. The wonderful world of "I could" invites our intelligent brain to investigate creative ways of dealing with things.

The fourth word is when we say **both** and instead of **either/or.** We're brought up with the idea to think the world is in two categories. Us or them. Right or wrong. Good or bad. We're really connected, we're really one, and when we realize that we need to cooperate, that's a big difference.

The fifth is actually a sentence. If we could all just learn it, we would likely have world peace instantly. It's *that* powerful. The sentence is "**what works for my tribe and your tribe for now and the future.**" Most people say instead, **"what's good for my tribe in the here and now."**

Next, we say **energy** instead of **fear** or **anxiety.** Anxiety and fear are what our ancestors had to manage when they lived in caves. They were in danger all the time – just about everything outside, from the wildlife to the weather, could kill them.

When we say energy, we realize that we can *think* about things. We can look for a way to problem-solve rather than fight or flee, neither of which is appropriate.

The last is a skill that says instead of **emergency**, we say **urgently.** The truth is, unless we work as cops, EMTs, firefighters, or coastguards, we rarely have genuine emergencies on our hands. Today we act as though we do, though, because our body is built that way.

Life in the 21st century can be pretty high pressure, leading to people growing frustrated when they have to wait. The whole body changes when this happens. We get energized and want to do something – usually fighting or striking out.

If we instead say *urgency*, we realize it's either high, medium, or low. If we really stop to think, almost everything we face is actually of very low urgency. It's hardly like we need to worry about bumping into a saber-toothed tiger while tending the lawn.

The modern version of the golden rule is to love yourself with an abundance that overflows to enrich the world. If the parents that come to our sessions can learn to do that, and model that for their kids, it teaches self-esteem. This, in turn, helps kids become bully proof. In addition, they have another tool to share with peers – and even bullies.

There is no denying that kids with high self-esteem are the best at bully proofing. When you really like yourself, you're not so dependent on what other people think or say about you. As a result, it's almost impossible for a bully's spiteful and unnecessary comments to gain the desired impact.

The Apexx of Bully Proofing

Doug Rankin is the Chief Vision Officer for Apexx. Apexx is a child development center that uses the tools of martial arts, fitness, after-school, and summer camp to have a positive impact on children's lives.

Doug and his team have enjoyed the privilege of working with thousands of children and adults to help put their lives on a better course. Doug is a two-time #1 bestselling author and a 6th Black Belt in Taekwondo.

We asked him what he thought the best things that kids can do to build their self-esteem and focus, and here's what he said.

"I would tell you the most important things that kids can do to build their self-esteem and focus are to make sure they get into a martial arts program.

The character development skills that they develop by learning martial arts help them obtain both short-term and long-term goals. This single skill is absolutely irreplaceable.

There is a virtual laundry list of benefits kids gain in their martial arts classes that they can integrate into their everyday lives.

For example, in martial arts, they are taught positive belief patterns so they can learn that they can accomplish things they set their minds and hearts towards.

This brings us to the discipline aspect of it is really the big thing that plays into it, because we can take the discipline that the children are learning, and then they apply it to themselves so that they're able to become better, stronger leaders overall because of their martial arts programs.

I also believe that it's true that kids who show better focus and self-esteem are less at risk for bullying or getting picked on. Self-esteem is proven to be one of the number one factors in bully prevention itself.

The way a kid walks, their posture, how they carry themselves – all of those things. How they feel about themselves and their self-worth really all starts at the beginning of their training and gets better from there.

So, in my opinion, it makes sense for parents who are reading this book to find a martial arts school around them to get their kids started at least on the path of building their self-confidence."

This leads to the next question. How do we tell the good martial arts schools from the bad martial arts schools?

"That's a fairly easy answer. The truth is, we have the first avenue of being able to check reviews on things like Google and Facebook, and Yelp. This gives insight into what other people are experiencing.

Getting referrals firsthand from friends or family that may have trained there. If they're comfortable with their martial arts school, they'll tell other people that they're comfortable with it as well.

The next logical step would be to go try out that martial arts program for yourself. Most reputable schools offer a short-term offer, whether that be a free week, or two, or at the very least a free lesson trial.

Be wary of schools that won't let you watch the class. There's no big, magical mystical secret about the martial arts, so if someone doesn't let you watch their classes, you are definitely in the wrong place.

Do be sure to go in and watch a class and check it out. What you see on the floor is what your child will end up doing and being, so you definitely want to be comfortable and meet the instructor.

That transparency should be available through all aspects of that martial arts school. You want to have a conversation with him or her and watch a class to see the students.

You may also want to avoid schools that are only open part-time. Personally, I'm always looking for a business owner who is solely invested in their business and one who is looking to help as many people as possible in their local community.

Here's why: one of the biggest inspirations I have is one student of ours whose name is Cathy. She started with me when she was 13 years old and I always said that Cathy was my poster child. She came in the door unable to look people in the eye. She was very shy and introverted. She gave me a nickname because she couldn't pronounce my name, so she called me, 'Mr. Sir.'

That was eight years ago, and now just this past week she got a job at the beach in speech pathology. She's also got her black belts with me and earned a master's degree. She had so many job offers she had lots of choices between places virtually across the entire United States.

Cathy is really one of the biggest inspirations that I can really say, hey, this is what martial arts can do for you in school. It can take this bashful, shy girl who really has no confidence or self-esteem and build her up into a master's degree.

And the accomplishment that it took for her to get to that point, the hard work, the effort, and the martial arts played a big part in that. I've had many conversations with her parents, and they say that very thing. Is that 'hey, you played a huge role in her life in getting her to the point that she is,' which makes me feel great.

The martial arts just flat out works, and it doesn't matter if you are young or old, male or female. The benefits gained from active training go far beyond the dojo walls."

The School Principal

Houn Hib is the Principal of Warm Springs Elementary School. With over 20 years in the education field, his expertise is immense. Houn also holds a master's degree, along with a doctorate in organizational leadership.

Houn shows other companies how organizations are run, working with and studying Fortune 500 companies and different types of high-level organizations. He is also in the trenches himself, working hand-in-hand daily with the students and doing his best to improve their academic achievements regardless of their socio-economic background.

Houn has a true passion for helping students become what they're supposed to become through academics, personally and socially. We got a chance to talk to Houn about the epidemic of bullying, how it impacts and affects kids, and how his radically different approach is changing lives for the better. Houn has a very different outlook than 90% of other schoolteachers and administrators, and he shared some of those insights

First and foremost, Houn says that bullying is an epidemic. Although this take is controversial, Houn *is* on the front lines of the schools every day. He says there are too many parent groups and people that feel that you should just teach a child to ignore bullies. He is not a big fan of that approach.

Houn believes that it's important to help teach a child the skills, tools, and abilities to deal with the bully verbally and physically. Although ignoring is one of the first steps, unfortunately this approach rarely works in the longer term.

Houn is quick to point out that he is *not* advocating to go punch and beat up kids who bully others! Rather, he is advocating for kids to stand up for themselves the *right* way. This means developing coping skills that will help them socially and emotionally.

He uses a recent example of an incident at his school. A child had been bullied for a long time. In this day and age, as cyber-bullying manifests more and more, the bullying doesn't stop when the school bell rings either.

As an administrator, he has to deal with the consequences through the education code. The child who is the aggressor gets a suspension. But Houn also deals with the victim – in this case, talking them through their experience and reinforcing that it's not their fault. He also gives them new tools and abilities to speak up and stand up for themselves, even at school.

He reminds them that if they, for some reason, punch the other kid after multiple days of bullying via the social media networks or even in person, that he, the school administrator is okay with that.

Houn goes on to say that, "I don't want to suppress just natural emotion of feeling like I need justice. However, our overall concept at the school is to restore peace after the incident is done. Once the aggressor has been dealt with through discipline, I consider the scales of justice balanced."

Houn also suggests bringing both sides in after the fact, allowing the victim to express their hurt. As you may recall, we do not necessarily think this is *always* advisable at Bully Proof Life, but it's certainly an option if both parties are receptive.

Houn prefers this two-fold approach – the restoration of justice and helping kids deal with raw emotion so they can see it from the victim's point of view. To let them know that it's *okay* that they felt hurt, they felt pain, and they unleashed themselves.

Houn says, "For me as an educator, the important part is teaching them the proper way of dealing with it. Either speaking to an adult, taking karate, or being involved in something positive and character building. Doing some type of extra-curricular activity allows them to be firm and assertive in the right way. What I enjoy talking about is kids being able to stand up for themselves, but also to be physically fit."

He believes all school administrators and educators should see the value in the health of kids at their facilities because he says it is no accident how bullying can relate to their self-esteem.

Dozens of studies have shown that bullies will tend to pick on kids that seem weak or timid or shy or not sure of themselves. That lack of self-confidence is like a drug for a bully, empowering them even more.

Of course, Houn is a proponent of physical fitness, having played college football himself. He knows firsthand that in the world of education, kids who are involved in regular extra fitness-based curricular activity tend to score higher on any kind of achievement test. When they're fit, they tend to be more alert, and their brains function much higher.

What's interesting about this is that it doesn't matter what socio-economic background you come from. Houn cites this example.

"In our school district, the superintendent promotes that we have a PE teacher who does fitness throughout the whole year for our school. We are big believers in that concept. I go a little further. As a principal, I try to find different ways of bringing people on campus to promote different types of fitness. Karate, or football, or any activity of that nature.

The kids who are more involved in a group activity or sports and fitness tend to be more assertive, tend to develop those leadership skills and abilities that kids who are more reserved, who don't join, who don't do physical fitness, tend to be."

Houn says that he believes that kids who are less assertive, who don't work out, or at least get involved in something … they tend to be victims of different types of bullying.

The fact is 92% of kids that get picked on fall into one of two categories. They either exhibit low self-esteem, or they're physically unfit.

So, that's why it's critically important for parents to get their child involved in a positive sport or activity such as martial arts. If not this, at least *something* at their school where they're going to stay physically healthy, engaged, and active.

Make Physical Activity Part of Your Child's Life

Many physical activities fall under more than one type of exercise. This makes it possible for your child to do two or even three types of physical activity in one day!

For example, if your son is on a basketball team and practices with his teammates every day, he is not only doing a vigorous-intensity aerobic activity but also bone-strengthening. Or, if your daughter takes martial arts lessons, she is not only doing vigorous-intensity aerobic activity along with mind focusing and confidence-building skills but also muscle- and bone-strengthening! Plus she's getting bully proof.

It's easier than you might think to fit each type of activity into your child's schedule – all it takes is being creative and finding activities that your child enjoys.

As a parent, it is important to help shape your child's attitudes and behaviors toward physical activity. Throughout their lives, encourage young people to be physically active for one hour or more each day, with activities ranging from informal, active play to organized sports.

Here are some ways you can do this:

- Go for a walk

- Go for a bike ride

- Skateboard

- Rollerblade

- Ice Skate

- Play catch in the yard

- Play tag

- Play hide and go seek

- Have a picnic in the park and play frisbee

- Go to the beach

- Go to the mountains

- Mow the grass

- Rake the leaves

- Pull weeds

- Plant flowers

- Plant a tree

- Dance

- Play hopscotch

- Badminton

- Ping pong

- Pool (the game)

- Pool (swim)

- The lake or the river (more swimming)

- Play handball

- Hockey (all kinds)
- Gymnastics
- Ballet
- Baseball
- Basketball
- Football
- Soccer
- Volleyball
- Golf
- Martial arts (of course)

There are countless more ways to keep your whole family moving. My apologies if I missed some of your current favorites. Be sure to let me know how your family stays active!

Make physical activity part of your family's daily routine by taking family walks or playing active games together. Give your children equipment that encourages physical activity.

Take kids to places where they can be active, such as your nearby martial arts studio, public parks, community baseball fields, or basketball courts.

Be positive about the physical activities in which your child participates and encourage them to be interested in new activities.

Above all, *make physical activity fun.*

Fun activities can be anything your child enjoys, either structured or non-structured. The martial arts provide a cool way for kids to stay active while maintaining a healthy lifestyle.

Other activities can range from team sports or individual sports to recreational activities such as walking, running, skating, bicycling, swimming, playground activities, or free-time play.

Instead of watching television after dinner, encourage your child to find fun activities to do on their own or with friends and family, such as walking, playing chase, or riding bikes.

An important note to all parents:

Set a positive example by leading an active lifestyle yourself. Whether you realize it or not, you are a leader – a leader of your family. Mother or father, it makes no difference.

Your children love you more than anything on this planet. They look up to you. They watch you and copy your behaviors and attitudes. When they are young, you are their first love, their first hero, and the leader they aspire to be.

Rise up to that expectation because they are counting on YOU!

The point is, no excuses. Just make it happen.

Do you ever find yourself saying any of the following?

- I am too busy with work
- I don't have the time, there is housework to do
- The weather is bad – it's too hot, or it's too cold
- It might rain later
- I have a headache
- The car has been acting up
- I blame the economy, politics, the neighbors next door…
- This isn't the time, we'll start tomorrow, next week, next month, next year…

All the responses are the same. They're just another excuse to justify an inactive lifestyle. Stop making excuses and start making adjustments.

You've got this!

Bonus: martial arts is one of the few sports that is great for the entire family. You can all train together to become more confident, fitter, and – best of all – become bully proof.

Let's go!

I'm Being Bullied. Now What?

According to a study conducted by the OLWES Bullying prevention program, one of the best tools that schools have for decreasing the problems associated with bullying behavior is to implement evidence-based prevention programs. As we all know, bullying can have serious effects during the school years. This, in turn, carries over into adulthood.

How do students and adults respond to bullying?

One indicator that shows how well schools are addressing bullying is the degree to which students indicate others in the school (fellow students and adults) respond appropriately to bullying. A minority of students report that fellow students frequently try to stop bullying, and this number decreases in higher grades. Students report that teachers are much more responsive than students when they witness bullying, although this number also decreases in higher grade levels.

What are the ways in which students are most often being bullied?

Many types of behaviors can be classified as bullying if the behaviors meet the definition presented earlier. Students are asked about the frequency with which they are bullied in ten different ways, which are summarized here:

- **Verbal:** the student is called mean names or teased in a hurtful way.

- **Rumors:** the student is the target of false rumors or lies.

- **Exclusion:** the student is left out on purpose or completely ignored.

- **Sexual***:* the student is bullied with words or gestures having a sexual meaning

- **Racial***:* the student's race is the focus of the bullying

- **Physical:** the student is hit, kicked, or pushed

- **Threat:** the student is threatened or forced to do things against his or her will.

- **Cyber:** the student is bullied via a mobile phone or another electronic device.

- **Damage:** the student has personal property taken or damaged

Students are most often bullied by being called mean names (verbal), having false rumors spread about them (rumors), or by being left out on purpose (exclusion).

Where are students bullied?

Both boys and girls are most often bullied at school in very public places, such as the playground/athletic fields, lunchroom, hallways/stairwells, and in class – with or without the teacher present. In all of these locations, the potential exists for many other students and teachers to be present.

This finding suggests that students and educators may benefit from more training about how to observe, identify, and react to a bullying situation.

Using a comprehensive bullying prevention program may help students and teachers recognize acts of bullying behavior and learn techniques for how best to help the bullied student.

Compared to boys, girls report being bullied more frequently in the lunchroom, in hallways/stairwells, and in the classroom. Boys report being bullied more frequently in gym class or the locker room/shower than girls. Of high school students who both bully and are bullied, half dislike school.

Who do students tell about being bullied?

Among almost all students, siblings or friends are most likely to serve as confidantes about the bullying, followed by parents or guardians (see figure 21).

Teachers or other adults at school are the least likely to be told that a student is being bullied. Girls are more likely than boys to tell siblings/friends or parents/guardians.

Of particular concern are the numbers of boys and girls who do not tell anyone about being bullied.

Boys are more likely than girls to have told no one. For both boys and girls, the percentage who tell no one increases substantially as they get older.

Siblings or friends are the people students are most likely to confide in about being bullied.

One of the best ways to help students help others, as well as to reduce the overall prevalence of bullying, is to implement a schoolwide anti-bullying program.

Even I Was Bullied

Today, I am a 9th degree black belt, a four-time national champion, a celebrity motivational speaker, and a movie star. But it wasn't always like that.

Here's my story.

When I was in junior high school, I was very short for my age. Of course, all of my friends started to grow much sooner and much faster. In fact, I was a very late bloomer. When I was in 7th grade, I was only three feet eleven inches tall!

I had friends at the time who were four and a half feet, five feet tall. When we got to eighth grade, I had grown a couple more inches. Unfortunately, some of my classmates and friends shot all the way to almost six feet.

Being the smallest guy in the room led to me getting picked on quite a bit. Thank goodness I had already been training and knew martial arts. Not because it meant I could fight and kick butt. The confidence, discipline, and self-esteem of the martial arts saved me from going into a shell and having a complete meltdown, though.

Now, at this time, I was also a little chunky because I hadn't grown. Naturally, kids being the mean little bastards they can be, I was picked on and made fun of because I was short and a little plump. One of my supposed friend's favorite things to call me was an Oompa Loompa (rent Willy Wonka and the Chocolate Factory from Amazon if you're too young to understand that reference.)

Again, my mental discipline from the martial arts training is what helped me and carried me through those times. It didn't stop people from picking on me, but it *did* allow me to have enough self-confidence and self-esteem to know that things would get better. Later in life, I would be very thankful for that. Obviously, I wasn't very happy at the time, though. Nobody likes being picked on, even kids that grow up to play Batman in the movies.

As we got into high school, I was just a little over five feet tall. When I got into high school, the upper classmen did a lot of hazing, which was pretty common in those days. At our high school, one of the many things that the seniors liked to do to the freshman was to try and pick them up and put them in trash cans.

Of course, on my third day of high school, this almost happened to me – though they didn't quite make it because I had enough skill to escape. I didn't fight them or hit them, but I did run and get away. Escape and defense were lessons learned from my martial arts training, so again, I was very thankful for that.

The attempted hazings continued – not just on me, but on many freshmen. One day I decided I wanted to try out for the wrestling team. Red Dragon Karate, which is our style of martial arts, is a form of MMA that incorporates judo, a Japanese discipline known for its great throwing, ground holds, and takedowns, so I figured that wrestling was right up my alley.

The biggest guy on our wrestling team was a real heavyweight. He was a senior named Brian. Word got out on the wrestling team that I was in the martial arts and that I knew karate, which at the time was still a mystery to most Americans. This was well before *Ninja Turtles*, *Power Rangers,* or *Mortal Kombat* were part of the pop culture landscape

So, our senior heavyweight wrestler decided he was going to try and see what this little karate kid could do. This was the day that the bullying stopped, purely accidentally. I don't know what his real intent was, but clearly, he wanted me to show everybody that I either knew martial arts or I didn't.

People had talked about how my Dad owned the local karate school in our town, so he put two and two together and figured out the name was related to me. He asked me to do a kick, but I didn't want to. One of the first things we learn in martial arts is to not show off or showcase our skill. Besides, I was still pretty shy and nervous. This was my first day out on the wrestling mats in the gym.

Brian kept goading me. "Just show me a kick, show me a kick, show me a kick," was seemingly all he could say. All the other wrestlers on the team were there – freshmen, sophomores, juniors, seniors – because it was day one orientation. I eventually agreed to do a kick, if only to stop him from running his mouth and causing a scene.

Now, Brian was six feet two inches tall and well over 200 lbs. While by contrast, I was just a little over four feet tall and weighed just shy of 100 lbs.

Brian held up his hand as high as his head and explained that he wanted me to kick it. I decided upon a roundhouse kick, which was at the time one of my favorite moves. He held up his hand, and I said, "Okay, I'll do this, and then you've got to leave me alone."

I went to do the kick, but unfortunately, he was holding his hand very close to his face. You can probably guess where this story is leading – I missed my target. It got as high as his outstretched hand, but my kick landed directly on his cheek, making a clapping sound that seemed to echo around the entire hall. Suddenly the gym that had been buzzing with conversation and excitement became deathly quiet. You could literally hear the proverbial pin drop. I thought he was going to kill me!

Instead, Brian looked at me, smiled, rubbed his cheek a little, and said, "that was a good kick!" From that day, we became friends, and he kind of took me under his wing. What's more, something else happened at that moment – pretty much all the bullying stopped.

Maybe that was because I gained the respect of the biggest, strongest guy in the school – albeit completely by accident. I never set out to do it, and I was scared as hell when I kicked that guy in the face. I had no interest in using my training to hurt people then, and I still don't today.

So you see, whether you're a martial artist or not, bullying can happen to anyone, anywhere, at any time. I just happened to be in a position and a place in my life where things worked out for me by chance and a little skill.

It doesn't always work like that for everybody, and I don't recommend trying to kick the biggest, toughest guy at your school in the face! Remember, I set out not to do that — it was an accident that fortunately worked out in my favor.

Self Defense

This chapter is revised and updated from my previous book: Bully Proof Fitness.

There is a very common misconception most people have about martial arts – that is that they are designed to teach people how to be violent and beat people up. Actually, the opposite is true.

Being in the arts for the better part of 45 years has allowed me to see, learn, experience, and come to understand that martial arts were developed as a means of self-defense in order for people to be able to protect themselves from those who oppressed them.

The systemized art of fighting and protection of self goes back thousands of years. Many people assume its origins are from Asia, but according to the history of the martial arts on Wikipedia, *"the earliest evidence for specifics of martial arts as practiced in the past comes from depictions of fights, both in figurative art and in early literature, besides analysis of archaeological evidence, especially of weaponry. The oldest work of art depicting scenes of battle, dating back 3400 BCE, was the Ancient Egyptian paintings showing some form of struggle. Dating back to 3000 BC in Mesopotamia (Babylon), reliefs and the poems depicting struggle were found. In Vietnam, drawings and sketches from 2879 BC describe certain ways of combat using sword, stick, bow, and spears."*

In this book, we will focus on self-defense moves that are fast, efficient, and easy to master – and work well for both kids and adults. I can't promise that you'll be pulling off moves to rival Bruce Lee, but that's not what the martial arts are about. Remember, defense, not aggression.

Self-defense move: 3 Pushes

Three pushes is, in my opinion, one of the best and easiest self-defense and protection moves you can learn. It is so effective that it is the move I would choose to use if I had to defend myself.

That's a big statement – at this point in my life, I know literally thousands of martial arts moves! The one I would use to defend myself is right here on this page, though.

Three pushes is so effective for three reasons.

- It's easy to master
- It uses the opponent's strength against them
- it keeps a would-be attacker away from potentially grabbing or stabbing us

Three pushes takes its name from the number of moves, as well as the amount of times you will give a potential bully or would-be attacker the opportunity to leave you alone.

Since we are teaching self-defense, and not self-*offense*, our first movement and technique will have us moving backward (away) from a potential attacker.

When someone is approaching us, and we do not know their intentions or what they want, we aim to keep them out of our *Critical Distance Zone* (CDZ). The CDZ is our safe area. To find yours, simply extend your arm straight out in front of you, fingers extended. The tip of your fingers is the CDZ.

When a stranger is approaching you, never allow them to be closer to you than the distance of the tips of your fingers with arm extended. No matter how fast or strong you think you are, when somebody is inside your CDZ, your ability to protect yourself effectively decreases by 100%.

There is a law of physics that states that *action is faster than reaction.* Therefore, their ability to strike or grab you (the action) will always be faster than your ability to block or avoid it (your reaction) when they are inside your arm's length. This is true both for the beginner and the advanced learner.

BULLY PROOF TIP: Through extended training, you will become aware of this zone without sticking your arm out in front of you. Since you would look silly walking around like that, practice with a friend or family member in the meantime.

Have them approach you, and when they do, tell them to STOP when you believe they are in the zone. Then, just lift your hand – if your fingers can touch them, you did it. Continuous training of the zone creates a hypersensitivity of the space around you, giving an almost 'Jedi'-like awareness.

For our self defense move, we want you to begin in a natural stance, feet about shoulder width apart. As if you were standing there talking to a friend.

Place both hands up in a non-threatening manner; it should appear that you are raising your hands as though surrendering. The hands should be about as high as your head, not above. And in line with your head not extended in front of you.

As the potential attacker is approaching, take one step backward and ask, **loudly**, "What do you want?"

If they stop to answer, stand your ground, always remaining aware that they are *not* within your CDZ. If they continue to advance, take another step backward and announce, even louder this time, **"I DON'T WANT ANY TROUBLE."**

If they *still* continue to advance, take one final step backward and **firmly order** (not ask!) them to **STOP**.

BULLY PROOF TIP: <u>ALWAYS speak loudly</u> - this takes practice. You can be, and probably *will* be, scared when confronted by a would-be bully or attacker. This human emotion (fear) is perfectly normal. As we mentioned earlier, though, we need to manage our emotions. It's OK to be scared, but it is *not* OK to *sound* scared. Be afraid on the inside. <u>PRACTICE!</u>

Move backward three times, speaking loudly and clearly. This communicates to the attacker – and anyone around you – that you are *not* the bully, that you *are* trying to protect yourself, and that you *do not* want to fight.

We limit our backward movement to only three steps for a few reasons, one of which is space. You may be in a parking lot, in a building, or in a space that doesn't allow you to back up without running into something behind you. In addition, you don't want the attacker to back you into an area with no people, and therefore nobody to possibly help.

BULLY PROOF TIP: Sad but true, many people aren't in the business of helping strangers. When they see a possible threat, they may just keep walking and ignore it. With their faces in their phones, people are constantly caught up in their own augmented reality. That being said, if you need help, yell **"FIRE!"** Everyone wants to see a fire. Crazy but true.

If the attacker continues to advance towards you once you have exhausted the retreat and words, they are leaving you no choice but to defend yourself. From the hands up position, you will now execute the push block. This block is fantastic because it does not use force against force. This block allows a physically weaker opponent the ability to easily avoid a grab or a punch from a bigger, stronger attacker.

BULLY PROOF TIP: If you are right-handed, begin this three-move sequence with your right hand. Lefties, begin with the left hand.

Move 1 – to properly perform the block, use the palm of the hand and push whatever is coming at you away and across your own body.

Move 2 – as they approach again, or attempt to use one or both hands, take your opposite hand and push across your body with your other palm leading the way.

Move 3 – after you have blocked twice, you will finish with a strike we call the Palm Heel. This strike again allows a weaker defender to end the potential threat with one move.

To properly execute a Palm Heel Strike, slightly bend the fingers of the striking hand and fold the thumb slightly inward. Push the bottom part of the palm (closest to the wrist) forward, and strike straight ahead while tensing the palm area.

BULLY PROOF TIP: The Palm Heel strike is best thrown to the face, with the main target being the nose. The palm heel is a "one and done" move, so it is *not* a move to play with, only recommended as a last resort.

We strongly recommend that you not only practice this move, but that you seek the help of professional instructors who can guide you through more detailed training in self defense. Find them at: www.bullyprooflife.com

Attention: School Admins, Staff, P.T.A. & P.T.O.

We will gladly come to your school with our team to teach, train and empower your students with the safety program that has helped tens of thousands of kids become bully proof and safe.

See it at http://bit.ly/2bullyproof, then contact us on +1-800-928-6598 or via email: rdkceo@reddragonkarate.com

Summary, Implementation, and Action Steps: The BULLY PROOF Action Plan

My goal for you in this book is to motivate and inspire you to take action and help yourself and your family get bully proof *now*. It's possible when you *take action and implement*.

I know this to be true because, after training and teaching thousands of kids and their parents and serving nearly 100,000 customers in over 35 years of full-time teaching, I have *seen* it work. I wish that I knew twenty years ago what I've shared with you in this short book.

I know it's not easy to get motivated, start, and change some bad habits while maintaining your health, sanity, marriage, and relationship with your kids. Throw in staying balanced, happy, and having a sound spiritual life, and it's even harder.

However, it's entirely possible to take a few shortcuts that can – and will – get you results. You'll get faster, build more confidence, and have even more self-esteem without spending tons of time in a gym.

How? Just *start*. The sooner you start taking action and building momentum, the sooner you'll get stronger and be even more confident.

If all you did was just got your kids or yourself to be a little more confident, or maybe lose a few pounds, you are already a success. Momentum builds upon itself. It reminds me of a great quote, "*You don't have to be great to start, but you gotta start to be great.*"

I'm not telling you this to impress you, but to impress *upon* you how important getting started and staying motivated is – and it begins with getting into a mindset of belief. If you have a company or business, and you are ready to get started implementing these strategies by having us teach or train your team with our award-winning, **BULLY PROOF LIFE** program.

Yes, it happens to adults and in the workplace too. We dedicate an entire chapter to this in my first book: BULLYPROOF FITNESS. Please go to www.bullyprooflife.com to get started.

In closing, if you have not already done so, download the FREE BULLY PROOF APP. This app will help you stay focused on the path to more success for your entire family, all while becoming bully proof.

Now, get out there and implement, and keep me posted on your progress!

Chris

PS - be sure you visit me on Facebook, Instagram, YouTube, and post a comment or video about how much you like BULLY PROOF, OK?

Thanks and Acknowledgments

I'd like to thank and acknowledge a few thought leaders and innovators in the community who are also helping kids become bully proof, build character, and become leaders on their own. These champions continue to inspire and help others on this journey.

Louis D. Casamassa. My father, the founder of Red Dragon Karate who is and was my first martial art instructor as well as my first "superhero." He started our company way back in 1965, and today the Red Dragon Karate schools located in Southern California are widely recognized as the pioneers of the mixed martial arts movement as it is known today. Find out more: www.reddragonkarate.com

Rich Kohler and his Mission: Bully Proof program. Rich is an award-winning child safety expert and the creator of two theme-driven and "edutaining" safety programs, Mission Bully-Proof and the fantasy adventure child safety movie/program, Journey of the Steal-Proof Master. His programs are highly regarded and have helped tens of thousands of children all around the world stay safe. For more info: www.RKEmpowerment.com

Clement Goh and his Buddy Adventures program. Buddy Adventures is an online learning adventure that reinforces the same life skills, and traits parents want for their children, done in an interactive and enjoyable way. We use a unique storytelling system to get children role-playing healthy behaviors, learning martial arts moves and exercising instinctively. Buddy Adventures has a values-based 18-month curriculum for ages 3 to 8, live online sessions, and a course for parents to build a rock-solid bond with their children. We believe in being allies with parents to create a better childhood experience, forming stronger family bonds, with a relentless mission to positively impact 100,000 families by 2025. For more information, you can find us on www.buddyadventures.one

Jason Kifer: https://www.matchats.com/

Mat Chats is the only life skills development system on the planet that produces proven, tangible results. His easy-to-implement, incentive-based character education program works with any martial arts system. Martial arts school owners, instructors, parents alike love MatChats.com and the real-world lessons it instills in children (and the kids love it too).

Stan Lee & Sara Lee. Their series of children's books is a great resource to help young kids learn life skills and how to deal with strong emotions. With topics that include making friends, perseverance, self-control, and courage, it's a great way to help your child make progress on these topics. The colorful characters gain wisdom from their experiences and advice from the martial arts instructor. Check them out at www.adventuresofharryandfriends.com

Can I Please Ask You for a Favor?

If you enjoyed this book and found it useful, then I'd really appreciate it if you would post a short review on Amazon. I do read all the reviews personally so that I can continually write what people want.

Thanks for your support!

About the Author

Originally from Bethlehem, PA, Chris' father Louis D. Casamassa is the creator and founder of the Red Dragon style of Martial arts, which was founded in 1965.

Red Dragon is widely recognized as America's first true Mixed Martial Arts style. Chris' father moved the family to California in 1972 as his father wished to continue expanding their martial arts school in the warmth and sunshine of California.

Chris trained side-by-side with his father from the young age of 4 through adulthood, and as the Red Dragon company grew, Chris continued to expand both his martial art and his business ability. He knew that he was destined to not only help his father run the martial art studios but to help his father take them from a small-time business to a multimillion-dollar licensed operation.

Chris is currently a 9th degree black belt, and CEO of the fourteen Red Dragon Karate studios in southern California.

For Chris, though, it's not all about the money. He's raised over $50,000 for the Make a Wish foundation, and he is on the board of the Kid Smart Foundation.

A 501c3 California nonprofit, the Kid Smart Foundation's core purpose is to help at-risk children become better, more well-rounded members of their community through martial arts training. This helps the children mature into smarter adults that have developed leadership skills.

In addition, Chris has helped over 63,765 kids become "Bully Proof Certified" with the Red Dragon studios, his workshops, training seminars, and special events. He travels the world to get the message out to kids and parents so they can live a better life, free from bullying and violence. His goal is to help 1 million kids by 2025

Chris enjoys speaking, teaching, training, and inspiring business owners, trainers, students, and school owners around the globe on ways they can empower their students and supercharge their business.

He competed professionally on the North American Sport Karate Tour (NASKA), where he became a four-time national champion.

Chris has appeared in dozens of film and television shows. Including *Batman & Robin*, *Walker: Texas Ranger*, *Buffy the Vampire Slayer,* and many more. His signature role for his millions of fans around the world is Scorpion, the super-ninja from the hit *Mortal Kombat* films and TV series.

He lives in La Verne, CA, with his wife Michelle and their children Emily and Adam – both of whom are certified bully proof ninjas. Chris can be contacted at his website www.chriscasamassa.com or through any of his social media channels.

- Twitter – www.twitter.com/realmkscorpion

- Facebook – www.facebook.com/chriscasamassa117

- Instagram - www.instagram.com/bullyprooflife

Also by Chris Casamassa

- **Bully Proof Fitness** (2016) *The ultimate guide for parents on the battle against bullies and bellies and how to make your kids feel like a super ninja.*

- **Business Kombat** (2021) *A 5-step plan to building the business of your dreams without selling out*

Made in the USA
Columbia, SC
21 August 2024

40861370R00057